Learning How to Get Through It

THE REASONS AND THE SEASONS FOR THE EXITS AND ENDINGS

Ginger Grancagnolo, Ed.D., D.Min.

BALBOA
PRESS

A DIVISION OF HAY HOUSE

Balboa Press books may be ordered through booksellers or by contacting:

Balboa Press
A Division of Hay House
1663 Liberty Drive
Bloomington, IN 47403
www.balboapress.com
1 (877) 407-4847

Because of the dynamic nature of the Internet, any web addresses or links contained in this book may have changed since publication and may no longer be valid. The views expressed in this work are solely those of the author and do not necessarily reflect the views of the publisher, and the publisher hereby disclaims any responsibility for them.

The author of this book does not dispense medical advice or prescribe the use of any technique as a form of treatment for physical, emotional, or medical problems without the advice of a physician, either directly or indirectly. The intent of the author is only to offer information of a general nature to help you in your quest for emotional and spiritual well-being. In the event you use any of the information in this book for yourself, which is your constitutional right, the author and the publisher assume no responsibility for your actions.

Any people depicted in stock imagery provided by Getty Images are models, and such images are being used for illustrative purposes only. Certain stock imagery © Getty Images.

Print information available on the last page.

ISBN: 978-1-9822-1375-6 (sc)
ISBN: 978-1-9822-1374-9 (hc)
ISBN: 978-1-9822-1376-3 (e)

Library of Congress Control Number: 2018911871

Balboa Press rev. date: 10/02/2018

CONTENTS

DEDICATION

To my mother, Julia, beloved Mama Novena, who taught me so much about life through her presence, yet the greater lessons were truly revealed through her death and leaving. It is her heavenly presence that now guides me ever so brightly. I am so humbly grateful for our never-ending love.

ACKNOWLEDGMENTS

To Grandma Malanga, Albert, Jose, Angel, Mom, Dad, Nino, all beloved family and friends who have continued in their journey back into the Divine Presence. Your ways continue to reshape me. Each one of you has given me courage to become a greater version of myself every day, and my love for you continues to grow even deeper.

INTRODUCTION

*W*hat happens when we leave? I mean, what really happens when we leave anything or anyone? What happens when others leave us? Why is it that sometimes it can be so difficult? It can feel hard to leave a job, relationship, a family home, or even a party. This is definitely true in my family traditions. We call it the "long Grancagnolo goodbye." Any time we are together, regardless of the circumstance, it takes forever for us to say goodbye and eventually leave. It could be a party, wedding, wake, or funeral; we linger and linger as we are getting ready to leave. We actually can predict it! It seems like when it's time to leave, somebody starts to move around in the group in an attempt to say goodbye. Then we engage in a variety of conversations, kissing, hugging, and kissing and hugging again. This continues for an hour until somebody declares, "Let's go! The car is running!" Eventually we leave, savoring every moment as we then proceed to our cars. As soon as cars begin rolling, we start discussing the happenings throughout the ride home. Then, as if that weren't enough closure, most of us will call each other to make sure we got home safely! We either really love each other or just have issues about leaving. My guess is that it's probably a little bit of both!

Regardless of the root source for our particular concerns, doubts, attachments, or fears, exits can carry a variety of emotional baggage, both knowingly and unknowingly. Perhaps the truth about exits is that they are all natural, progressive, and necessary for our personal development. With every ending, there is the promise of a better beginning.

This ongoing process of endings linking to beginnings is as certain as each exhalation that gives way to the next glorious inhalation. It is the permanent cycle of life. Even though we innately know that this is the truth about life, we oftentimes remain unaware with regard to how we personally respond to endings that have occurred along the path of life. Sometimes we are too young to really comprehend the impact of specific experiences that can trigger emotional endings. As children, we may not be able to process the effects of leaving a best friend because of a family move, losing our first dog or cat, or the painful experience of losing a parent through divorce or death.

There are times when an experience may not have appeared to be so life altering, yet according to each person's interpretation and reaction, it can create a significant roadblock that subsequently derails that individual's ability to successfully follow a heartfelt dream, goal, or passion for the future. Some examples of such obstacles that can easily detour our life paths can be an unexpected pregnancy, a DWI that mars a resume, a family illness that drains a prospective star athlete's college fund, or a necessary family move that forces friendships to come to an abrupt or unwanted separation.

Endings and exits can be difficult. They arrive with and without warning, and they will always affect us. Some endings can be planned, such as a retirement or the last days of a terminally ill loved one who was able to designate specific plans for his or her funeral arrangements. However, the potency of each closure is not in the planning; it is in the allowing of the process itself. Even if an ending is evident, the process always carries a divine script that only an open and contrite soul can readily embrace.

All endings and exits, regardless of how or when they occur, are connected to lessons about control, trust, letting go, abandonment, and ultimately death itself. All endings and exits carry blessings of great joy and wisdom that can gently reshape our thoughts, beliefs, behaviors, and choices as we are guided out of fears and into the loving divine truths inherent in our experiences. Every ending and exit has the potential to lift us out of any false belief in limitation so that we can reclaim our endless ability to recreate ourselves into the highest version of who we truly desire to become.

With every ending and exit, a new beginning can become the powerful threshold for greater joy, forgiveness, adventure, or faith if we can allow the process to become our sage guide, physically, emotionally, mentally, and spiritually. Willingness to change is the key switch whenever we find ourselves about to pivot out of one phase of life and into another. As we become more and more willing to let the specific ending bring us into the new beginning, we can be reborn into a richer and more fulfilling life, realizing a deeper feeling for the ancient truth, "Life goes on."

The purpose in this writing is to reveal the ongoing process that has happened and will continue to happen throughout our life's journey. We will review and reexamine our experiences literally from birth to death. As we embrace each juncture point of importance, we will be able to reclaim the fruits in each rite of passage, which will thereby give us a greater meaning and value for who we have become. We will rediscover the loving hand of God lifting or carrying us over the troubled waters of our lives in ways that we may never have noticed before.

Through these chapters, we will be able to recommission

ourselves as the true co-creators we were intended to be. Together with the innate power of the Holy Spirit, we will be better able to make sense out of the "Why did that have to happen?" question about our past, so that our futures can become more invigorating and free, regardless of what may have developed thus far.

The intent of this writing is to open our senses to the natural cycle of life, feeling God's hand in ours leading us into the beautiful and fulfilling life He has prepared for us, if we would just be willing to change whatever we think already happened and make way for the infinite possibilities for a heartfelt greater way of living and loving.

As each chapter unfolds, we will be able to reflect upon the various aspects of our lives. With this in mind, it is recommended that a journal be used to record personal feelings regarding the focus within each chapter. There is no need to rush through the chapters. Take your time. Enjoy. Enjoy your life—then, now, always. Remember: life goes on!

> The Lord is my shepherd,
> I shall not want;
> He makes me to lie down in green pastures.
> He leads me beside still waters;
> He restores my soul.
> He leads me in the path of righteousness
> For His name's sake.
> Even though I walk through the valley of the shadow of death,
> I fear no evil.
> For thou art with me;
> Thy rod and thy staff, they comfort me.
> Thou prepare a table before me

In the presence of my enemies.
Thou anoint my head with oil,
My cup overflows.
Surely goodness and mercy shall follow me
All the days of my life
And I shall dwell in the house of the Lord, forever.

-Psalm 23:1–6

PART ONE

Earthly Exits

CHAPTER 1

Born to Lose

s the story of anyone's life begins, it is certainly overflowing with so many possibilities. Each one of us carries the ongoing promise of a progressive evolution. Each one of us can be the continuation of our heritage, culture, and endless hopes, wishes, and dreams. Our parents may have even expressed these expectations to us at various times over the course of our lives.

Yet truthfully, not every life may have had such formidable beginnings. Some of us may have had a rocky start as we entered into this earthly dimension because our mothers may have experienced an unsettling pregnancy. In any event, the overlay of life's contrasting polarities can be exhibited in its tensions and dualities even before we are born.

Life is a miracle. Being born into our physical bodies is a constant wonder. The process of invisible and visible energies coming together with an innate rhythmic unfolding, precise in every detail, every cell, every finger, toe, and eyelash, is and always will be an unfathomable miracle. God is at Her gracious best having tenderly shaped and fondled us into very specific individuals. And somehow over the divinely designed formula of approximately nine months, we move out of the spirit dimension and into the physical dimension, while maintaining the full potency of spirit, to become our unique selves. Life, our living, breathing selves, is always a miracle.

To further highlight the commingling of two of the dimensions, it is vital to state the main principle of life itself. All life is energy, both seen and unseen. All life is energy vibrating at various frequencies. At our core, we are an unseen energy of spirit, which is the divine umbilical cord to the Source of Everything—that is, the Universe, God. *Wow!* A miracle! Our physical form is a specific expression of God with a very specific creational blueprint and fingerprint. Each individual carries the whole of the source within him or her, while simultaneously expressing a particular aspect of God, which we call personality. This magnificent ongoing union of the All of the Everything That Is, expressing itself through each particular person, can be stated in both scientific and spiritual terms with equal accuracy. Scientifically, this principle is stated as "Energy can neither be destroyed nor created, only transformed." Spiritually, this same principle can be stated as "made in the image and likeness of God."

The proof of the continuous evidence of dualistic dimensions simultaneously existing is also reinforced by the fact that 99 percent of all humanity's DNA is exactly the same. What an amazing revelation of our Creator's wisdom to keep us connected, yet unique, by a mere 1 percent difference. *Wow!* A miracle!

This miracle of our uniqueness, therefore, begins even before we are born. The womb experience is the best witness of our unity in the divine as each of us is becoming a particular person, with particular traits, talents, and characteristics. Throughout the pregnancy, we experience what is often described as the mystifying love experience. This is because during our time within the womb, all our needs are being satisfied without effort. We are fed, nurtured, safe, and protected. As we develop, we begin to individuate sounds and feelings. This first world of both physical and divine is, in fact, truly perfect. We feel the unconditional love of God while feeling connected to our biological mother and our soon to be next physical world with all of its promises and adventures. We are safe and loved. We are the balance of human and divine waiting to be born. *Wow!* A miracle!

Even though these initial nine months of life seem so perfect, the downside, of course, is that we will leave the womb and, for the first time, actually experience loss. As we leave the mystifying security of God's love and mother's love, we are met with an onslaught of sensory stimulation. New sounds, voices, temperatures, all kinds of movements bombard our tiny bodies, creating a new script for this unfamiliar environment, as we hear for the first time, "It's a boy!" or "It's a girl!"

Our first reaction to this physical dimension in our new little bodies may have been, "Where am I? This doesn't feel like the womb." As those first moments of our lives unfold, we actually experience a loss. Our souls, still and always connected to the Source, are wondering why this doesn't feel like heaven!

In those first moments, the duality of our life's path begins. In order to get somewhere, we are going to have to leave someplace or someone. These feelings, although stored deep within our consciousness, are often not able to be readily accessed or realized until a much later time along the journey. This fundamental experience can actually become an unconscious compass during the earliest stages of our lives.

From womb to birth to about two years of age, our first lessons about becoming who we are pivot from the first exit point of having to leave the womb. During these early years, our focus of development is simply upon being safe. Are we warm, cold, hungry, tired, in need of touch? These needs translate into the cornerstone lesson of safe versus unsafe on our earthly journey. As newborns and infants, we begin to store up information about getting our needs met in order to maintain safety. We learn which sounds, cries, and volume of tones can solicit the best response for our needs at any given time.

Through the course of these initial years, we learn who responds, who doesn't, and how it feels. The lesson of contrast is very essential for future building blocks of proper discernment, and no judgment or blame is implied here.

The impact of our first loss, leaving the womb, is what sets up this next lesson of safe versus unsafe, and it is meant to get us started upon the earthly path that is already tainted with an abundance of yeses and noes that we have recorded by the age of two. We are rapidly compiling information that contributes to the safe versus unsafe lesson, as we are also learning to navigate our newfound arms, legs, and voice. In effect, we are doing whatever we can to recreate the womb experience in our new earthly environment. Our home and its surroundings are our new womb, and our focus is to make them feel as similar as possible, even though we are also engaged in the greatest adventure of curious exploration with every "What does this do?" and "What's this for?" that we become focused upon. Once again, the dualistic qualities of earth's conflicts continue. Sometimes we like what we find, and sometimes we don't. Sometimes those around us are agreeable to our purposes, and sometimes they are not.

At this stage and somewhere during the first two or three years, we learn through the first loss of leaving the womb and the first few years of infancy a major shift in awareness. The shift is this: When in the womb, we were one in total unconditional love. Upon leaving the womb, we became intertwined with endless conditions that, during the first two years, are enmeshed in issues of safe versus unsafe feelings.

The first loss of leaving the womb is actualized through seemingly unexpected experiences of being in a little body and making noises that hopefully will effectively produce safe and pleasurable results, perhaps in a feeble attempt to recreate our first home of mother's womb.

Our first exit out of the womb can create the illusory loss of unconditional love as we try to adjust to a world already complex with conditions. For some, this experience is very traumatic because they were surrounded by extenuating circumstances that weighed heavier on the unsafe side as opposed to the safe side.

For some, these first few years may have included an illness— their own or a significant other's—that may have diminished some experiences toward the easy feelings of safety.

On the flip side, some of us may have experienced very sound and comfortable beginnings. Regardless of the qualities of these first recordings, the effects remain stored as our initial understandings of safe versus unsafe and unconditional love versus conditional love. These recordings, combined with our first feelings of leaving the womb, become the pillar lesson for how we develop and integrate strategies to become who we were ultimately designed to be.

No matter what, our exit from the womb and seeming loss of safety will provide good space for a greater quality of understanding as our journey unfolds. Truly, as one door closes, as we will all too quickly learn, many more will close, and endless more doors will open. *Wow!* A miracle!

Remedy for learning and letting go:

* Sit quietly with your eyes closed.
* Create an easy rhythm for your breathing and allow all of your attention to be focused on the center of your chest, where you know your heart and soul to be.
* Sense a beautiful, gentle, golden light in the center of your chest that seems to radiate and increase with every inhalation and exhalation.
* Focus upon the pulsating golden light as you allow yourself to imagine a beautiful place where you feel totally free, calm, and safe. This place may be real or imaginary. This place will be referred to as your "safe haven."
* Remain in your safe haven and create as much detail as possible. Feel as if you are really there.
* Once you have created your safe haven, a being of light will make its presence known to you. This presence may be Father God, Mother God, Jesus, the Holy Spirit, or an assigned angel. From this point forward, this holy presence will always be waiting for you when you enter into your safe haven.
* Sit comfortably with the holy presence and review the following questions. Allow the holy presence to give an increase of awareness and insights.
* Examine these questions with the holy presence:
  - Were there any circumstances that occurred while I was in the womb that may have interrupted my ability to feel safe? Examples: troubled pregnancy; untimely or unwanted pregnancy; fear or emotional problems on the part of mother or father; addictions.
  - Were there any circumstances that occurred during my infancy and through the first two to three years of life that

may have interrupted my ability to feel safe? Examples: financial or emotional strife that limited the parents' ability to satisfy familial needs, divorce, relationship problems with parents, addictions in parents, absent parent due to work schedule or emotional inability to relate or connect, postpartum depression in mother, the need of another sibling due to disability or illness superseding attention to my needs, death of a family member that causes extended grief, and unavailability of parents to emotionally bond with me.

* Breathe, relax, and allow for any and all insights and awareness to increase your understanding concerning safe versus unsafe issues.
* Ask the holy presence to dissolve your interpretations, impressions, and false-premise residues that may have developed.
* Ask the holy presence to help you understand the divine purpose for any experiences and to fill your memories with glorious feelings of strength, peace, and victory.
* Hear and feel the holy presence repeatedly saying to you, "Remember, I am with you always, no matter what, even to the ends of the earth."
* Allow a loving embrace with the holy presence and say, "Thank you."
* It is suggested that you record these reflections in a journal for further review.

Before I formed you in your mother's womb, before you were born, I set you apart and appointed you as my prophet to the nations.
—Jeremiah 1:5

CHAPTER 2

First Exit

We always seem to cherish our early family photos. They clearly can tell so many stories. We laugh about our clothes, which appeared so stylish at the time. We take long gazes at the furniture and surroundings in an attempt to conjure up the stored memories of these early days. We treasure these photos regardless of who else is in them or the nature of the captured event because they might just hold a glimpse of who we were and how we became who we are now. Perhaps, with enough focus and reflection, we can look into our own young eyes and see or feel an emotion that may still be lingering within this present version of ourselves.

Those early years carry their own signature experiences and vital lessons. Even though we may not think we remember them, those years shaped us and created another fundamental aspect of who we are today.

Somewhere between the ages three to six years old, we experienced the first exit. By this time, language is obvious and oftentimes increasing rapidly with each passing day. And even if we didn't exactly understand what all these adventurous sounds truly meant, we clearly were learning how their usage influenced others around us, as well as how we could further secure getting our needs met.

The acceleration of language ultimately prompted the lesson of our first exit. The lesson of first exit was centered around leaving our second womb, which was our home, in order to go to school.

The lesson of first exit was markedly categorized by truly leaving the home and going into a very different environment. Even though birth itself moved us into a new environment, the focus of this initial state was to provide safety and love as close to the womb-like experience as possible. As we became language literate enough, we left the comforts of home and now had to learn how to adapt to a totally unfamiliar place, with unfamiliar people, peers, and conditions.

The lesson of first exit actualized by going to school triggered a sense of loss that may or may not have been expressed. Somewhere inside, we got the message that life might not be just about us and our needs. Somewhere during preschool and first or second grade, we were faced with a brand-new set of circumstances that we may or may not have expected. We had to leave our families and their routines. We had to trust and listen to other adults while learning to follow rules and acclimate to boundaries and conditions with others our own age.

The first exit lesson clearly sent a different message than learning how to recapture the safety of the mystical love experience within the womb. Now, through the first exit lesson of leaving the nest and going to school, we had to learn the seedlings of independence.

The impact of the first exit lesson illuminates our evolutionary process once again. During this time frame, we had to learn to accept the conditional ways of living on earth. Prior to this time, we had clear feelings of unconditional heavenly existence. We could just be, and everyone around us would adapt to us and our needs. As we began to speak and use our words more fluently, we also lost the unconditional script from whence we came.

As we left the nest to go to school, we subtly experienced the loss of heaven as our home. Our souls remember this true abode always, but its full front and apparent vision faded into the subconscious in order to allow the natural stages of development to systematically unfold. The experience of school from three to six years of age announced to our inner being the necessity of learning the way of earthly living. We learned at this early age the values of competition and cooperation, joining in and being left out, responsibility and its consequences. For the first time, through the first exit lesson of leaving home and going to school, we may or may not have learned that we are a part of something bigger than ourselves. We may or may not have learned that performance and accountability, although difficult at times, can be the cornerstone gem for the future that could make us shine through self-motivation instead of waiting to be motivated.

The first years of education created a microcosm of life itself. We had to adjust to a larger hierarchy of authority while assimilating the beginning concepts of self-acceptance and self-worth based on how well we succeeded.

During the first exit lesson, we began the process of learning how to become individuals through the interaction with and reflection of others. This lesson, of course, is a never-ending process, yet the fundamental roots, both positive and negative, were planted at this early stage. Even at that age, we began to store memories about conditional living versus our original home of unconditional loving. This dualistic dilemma was the conflict we needed to push us forward. Life at any stage is always about going forward and becoming more than before. Without loss, leaving, and exits, no progress can ever be achieved. Without loss, leaving, and exits, we could never reclaim the infinite promise of the divine that we see carrying the spark of the eternal I Am. Each one of us was created to individually shine in a particular way, experiencing a specific gift that is an aspect of God. At every stage, we received guidance and experiences that were meant to help us remember who we really are. Even at the early stage of first exit, our souls recorded the needed information that would serve us for years and years to come, just like the joyful recollection as we discover a seemingly lost photo of our childhood. Whatever we thought we lost was actually recorded and stored within our subconscious, ready to be reclaimed and used for greater purposes somewhere in a future stage. Every leaving, even from this first exit, prepared us to become freer and greater than what any original experience could have ever predicted. The first exit paved the way for later strengths and opportunities, but we needed to learn how to leave our smallness and the limitations of our family home first. Leaving a small opinion of self to leap into a greater version of self may be the major lesson in the school of life that seems to repeat itself endlessly.

This first exit lesson in order to go to school may have given us the priceless lesson of becoming a lifelong learner regardless of our awareness at that time. The powers of learning, changing, and letting go will always be the precious gems for creating our best lives ever at any moment in time. And to think it started in the first classroom!

Remedy for learning and letting go:

* Sit quietly with your eyes closed.

* Create an easy rhythm for your breathing and allow all of your attention to be focused on the center of your chest, where you know your heart and soul to be.

* Sense a beautiful, gentle, golden light in the center of your chest that seems to radiate and increase with every inhalation and exhalation.

* Focus upon the pulsating golden light as you allow yourself to imagine a beautiful place where you feel totally free, calm, and safe. This place may be real or imaginary. This place will be referred to as your safe haven.

* Remain in your safe haven and create as much detail as possible. Feel as if you are really there.

* Once you have created your safe haven, a being of light will make its presence known to you. This presence may be Father God, Mother God, Jesus, the Holy Spirit, or an assigned angel. Remember, this holy presence will always be waiting for you when you enter into your safe haven.

* Sit comfortably with the holy presence and allow yourself to imagine a pleasant memory of early childhood between the ages of three and six years old. You may also recall a familiar photo.

* Allow yourself to feel what you might have been like at this early age. Do you feel happiness, joy, strife, sadness coming forth from that very young version of yourself? Simply observe your feelings and sense if you often still can feel these emotions now.

* As you remain reflecting upon this image of yourself, take a moment and recall any particular event that may have occurred during these years. Did you move? Did a parent need to leave home due to a change in career, illness in the family, or a separation or divorce? Did you lose a pet? Did a close neighborhood friend move away? Did a family member die?

* Allow some time to reflect upon these events and feelings so that you can recall how they may have impacted you and/or the family dynamics.

* Reflect upon how these events and emotions may have shaped your present-day confidence or self-image. Allow any feeling to simply bubble up so that you can choose to reevaluate who you are now with a greater sense of understanding.

* Be sure to ask the holy presence to guide you through these reflections so that you can feel the presence of divine wisdom helping you to reclaim a more confident sense of inner safety, peace, and self-worth.

* It is suggested that you record these reflections in a journal for further review.

Whom will he teach knowledge and to whom will he explain the message? Those who are weaned from milk, those taken from the breast? For it is precept upon precept, precept upon precept, line upon line, line upon line, here a little, there a little.

—Isaiah 28:9, 10

CHAPTER 3

Time to Reason

As we grew and adapted to our school life, a new routine for how we were to live got set up. The school calendar seemed to be the map for how our experiences unfolded. September had more significance as a new beginning than the true calendar new year of January 1.

We followed along with segments of learning through marking periods and looked forward to holiday events like Halloween, Thanksgiving, and Christmas, and to special school celebrations and activities, music, and sports programs. This next phase of learning, leaving, and letting go continued during the primary grades. During the ages of seven to about eleven, we experienced the lesson of learning how to use our reasoning.

Up until this point, we were not skilled or developed sufficiently enough to reason through our own decision-making processes. We mostly followed as instructed by parents, teachers, and other adults. This, of course, was not inherently positive or negative, but rather the building blocks needed to get us to the next stage. Certainly, we were not always compliant with rules or guidelines doled out by those with the voice of authority, and our responses may have been based on impulse or immediate satisfaction. The brain itself was not fully integrated enough at that time to allow us a logical thought process that might have used both inductive and deductive reasoning skills. In fact, the main focus of this next stage, "time to reason," was meant precisely to start the process of cultivating the essential mental and emotional acuity of logical and effective thinking that would produce positive and desirable results throughout our lives.

Through the stage of learning to reason, which extended approximately from age seven to eleven, we interfaced with a variety of dualistic situations. We might have challenged parents and those in authority with an often push/pull type of response regarding homework, chores, bedtime, self-care, and even how we "talked back" to those presenting the rules. These kinds of push/pull responses probably extended between and among siblings and peers. Even if you were an only child, random emotions wrapped the version of yes/no and affected your daily expressions.

During this stage, we were starting to participate in life with more individuality. We were perhaps exploring more of the feelings interwoven with personal power. For sure, young children have demonstrated their personal power before the age of seven. The notable point here is that at this stage of seven to eleven, we were meant to develop the beginnings of analytic processing so we could determine the value of cause and effect. We were meant to go through the process of watching what happens as a result of choices that we personally made and, even more importantly, learning to realize the consequences of a specific decision.

A simple example may be a common one. Somewhere during these years, we may have been assigned to complete a specific project by a specific date. It might have been a science project, studying for a test, or following guidelines regarding a sports activity, such as showing up for practice, caring for uniforms, or remembering permission slips.

When we were asked if requirements were met, we may have assuredly answered, "Yes, it's done." Meanwhile, the tasks at hand may have been done inappropriately, incompletely, or not at all. The procrastinated or ignored requirements may have resulted in failing grades, release from a team or event, or grounding by parents. These are mundane experiences, yet of vital importance if they were not understood and assimilated properly.

At this age phase, the brain and emotional components were able to comprehend the cause-and-effect relationship that in the younger years we were not able to grasp sufficiently. What was the key to this lesson between the ages of seven and eleven was the consistency of parental interaction for both positive and negative choices. Every choice made by us at that time was preparing us to learn how to trust our own thinking and ultimately how to trust the process of life based on cause and effect. We needed to be repeatedly reminded that our thoughts and choices created outcomes. Just like learning a formula, we needed reinforcement and steady guidelines to help us realize what happened when we kept our word and what happened when we didn't.

Through these years, discipline and support were meant to teach us how powerful we could be even from the smallest desire. Each desire coupled with a teachable moment could have paved the way toward ongoing confidence and evidence that we truly were created to make our dreams come true. The beginnings of any "dream-come-true life" started with how we learned to reason our way in or out of any circumstances.

Sometimes, we can make an assumption that past generations were more consistent in making children responsible for their thoughts and actions. Some may argue that past generations were too controlling with little regard for real supportive, teachable experiences. Some may state that although present generations may communicate more openly with their children, they create confusion in the natural development of reasoning, logic, and cause-and-effect relationship between choices and outcomes by being overprotective or lacking in follow-through and discipline, and this could allow for the dysfunctional pattern of entitlement.

Regardless of what our experiences were during the ages of seven to eleven and beyond, we were being shaped by how we reasoned with ourselves as we witnessed both positive and negative outcomes.

Reasoning, cause-and-effect thinking, and its consequences may have begun during our childhood, but they may also have created a fundamental pattern of personal empowerment and self-deserving factors that may be a detriment or blessing even to this day.

Reasoning and the awareness of cause/effect thought patterns are paramount to how we learned to apply and appreciate our endless human potential. Effective reasoning skills during the childhood stage were meant to build up an ongoing emotional and mental bank account that could result in very satisfying adult relationships because we learned early enough that we are responsible and accountable for our own actions and behaviors. Many adult codependent traps could have been avoided if we were held to the cause-and-effect reality check in our earlier years.

Accountability builds personal freedom and empowerment. It could take a lifetime of practice. In order to set the stage for this level of thinking and interacting, we had to learn how to let go of outgrown babyish emotional behaviors demonstrated in an "I want it, and I want it now" syndrome and develop a more appropriate "I want it and I am willing to do what's going to make it happen" attitude. We needed to leave the impatient, immediate-gratification-of-needs-impulse self and begin to observe and participate in the process of life itself, oftentimes learning great lessons of cooperation and compromise. These lessons were not easily achieved, and therefore consistency and support were also equally important.

If we were able to let go of the "me, me" vision of life that was no longer rational, a new and greater script was put more securely in place. The more effective behavior model allowed us to prepare and execute needs with better results and less drama, while we also learned how to function with others and still maintain a sense of self. The lesson was the seed for a lifetime of how to be *me* and still enjoy *we*.

We may or may not have been able to achieve this kind of letting go during those years because of surrounding situations, interferences, or interruptions. What is essential to remember, however, is that our soul always holds the curriculum in its perfection and entirety. Our soul is the timeless teacher. Through our quiet time, prayer, and meditation, our soul's wisdom can bubble up any needed correction or awareness adjustment so we can reassess any missing or confused life experiences that can set us back on track to clear and concise thinking. Our soul's wisdom can correct the past to empower the present and the future. Our soul's wisdom is the ultimate voice of absolute reason.

Remedy for learning and letting go:

* Sit quietly with your eyes closed.
* Create an easy rhythm for your breathing and allow all of your attention to be focused on the center of your chest, where you know your heart and soul to be.
* Sense a beautiful, gentle, golden light in the center of your chest that seems to radiate and increase with every inhalation and exhalation.
* Focus upon the pulsating golden light as you allow yourself to imagine a beautiful place where you feel totally free, calm, and safe. This place may be real or imaginary. This place will be referred to as your safe haven.
* Remain in your safe haven and create as much detail as possible. Feel as if you are really there.
* Remember, every time you are in your safe haven, the holy presence is always there waiting to guide, assist, and comfort you.
* Examine these questions with the holy presence and pause to reflect upon any insights or awareness.
  - Does any particular event, situation, or circumstance seem to be a highlighted experience at any time from the age of seven to about eleven?
  - How did it impact you positively or negatively?
  - Were you by yourself or with others?
  - Was it family, friends or school related?
  - What strong emotions did it bring up?
  - Did you feel empowered or disempowered?
  - Did any experience during these years alter your sense of confidence?

- Did you feel you experienced adequate or appropriate discipline and encouragement during these years?
- If so, how (both positively and negatively)?
- Did any situation during these years seem to abruptly change your sense of self or stability? Examples: a death, loss, hurt, abuse, addiction, divorce, or move to a new location.
- Ask the holy presence to illuminate your awareness about this time in your life. As the holy presence to give you insights as to how you did or didn't develop the beginning skills of cause-and-effect reasoning and how it has influenced you even into your present life.
- Ask the holy presence to correct your interpretations about experiences and how these experiences may have conditioned your ability for cause-and-effect reasoning.
- Ask the holy presence to clear and restore your sense for logical reasoning skills now, past, present, and future, so you can reclaim and assert all God-given wisdom.
- Ask the holy presence to reactivate your natural sense of accurate cause-and-effect decision making so you can remain positive in creating your optimum personal reality.

* Take your time reflecting upon these insights. It is suggested that you record these reflections in a journal for further review.

For you know that we dealt with each of you
as a father deals with his own child encouraging,
comforting and urging you to live lives worthy of
God, who calls you into his kingdom and glory.
—1 Thessalonians 2:11–12

CHAPTER 4

Struggling to Be Me

With each passing experience, adventure, failure, and victory, every year of our life carried a similar and thematic lesson. Every phase was designed to teach a balance of freedom, knowingly or unknowingly, to develop our own individuality while learning to integrate with others around us who were ultimately doing the same thing. This ongoing challenge began at birth and continued through interfacing with family members, to other parental figures, to early childhood peers, to other significant influences, such as coaches, teachers, and neighborhood residents.

From birth to somewhere around our preteen and teenage years, our inner compass was set to guide us toward becoming more comfortable as we explored who we were while adapting to our cause-and-effect choices and consequences. We also were simultaneously learning how to navigate through the cause-and-effect choices and consequences of others that might have interrupted the natural flow of development.

In truth, no one experienced a natural flow of learning to exit one phase of life and transition into another. The suggestion throughout the course of this missive is to help us review where we've been with regard to where we are now. When we reflect upon each stage of letting go of who we were, the main point for discernment is not that our transitions and letting go weren't perfect, but rather that we see value in our responses to events and situations that might have delayed, hindered, or confused us. This is the essential worth of being able to identify, remember, and review what has happened to us along the way for the purpose of reevaluating our reactions to life at any stage so that we can seek clearer awareness about who we became with a renewed trust in the divine healing wisdom that is ever-present with our souls.

Up to the adolescent stage, our awareness was probably not tuned into the wisdom of the soul due to the fact that we were mostly tethered to the standards, customs, and values of our families. Even within our families' own adhered-to dysfunctionalities, we knew following the tribe was the predominant way to maintain safety and security. In some ways, this certainly was necessary, since we were not mature enough to make our own rational decisions. Certainly, there were strong demonstrations of our budding willful spirits along the way, and again, what mattered most was how we steered through it. Did we progressively learn to trust ourselves and the tribe, or did we somehow sense a greater need for freedom of expression?

This push/pull for more personal freedom versus fear of leaving or being disapproved of by the tribe was the overall lesson during the adolescent stage. We probably struggled on both sides of this seesaw, not surefooted enough to understand the full dynamics of either side. For these reasons and more, the adolescent stage could be named a "struggling to be me" stage, which could begin around twelve or thirteen and run its bumpy course all the way through the early twenties, depending upon each individual and circumstance.

At this stage, the tug-of-war for us was both internal and

external. At that point, we were already quite loaded with so many *shoulds* and *should nots* while feeling the increased desire for the taste of freedom. Our internal database was programmed with standards for success, traditions, religion, sex, financial and political views, values about authority, family ties, and relationships, just to name a few. Both consciously and subconsciously, we carried an invisible template about these areas of life and how our tribe viewed or judged the interactions within society and the world. Mostly, we absorbed preconceived notions about these issues with little or no personal discernment. At the time, we may not have needed to sort it all out yet in order to feel safe, because most of our safety needs were already being met from within the tribe.

As we entered the adolescent stage, we began to desire more and more freedom of expression, decisions, and explorations of life itself. These desires were natural and necessary. The conflict and ongoing tug-of-war arose when we took action upon these desires while risking retaliation from the imposed tribal mind of family mores. We feared letting go as well as feared feeling confined. The struggle was further compounded if our issues from earlier stages were not sufficiently learned or resolved.

For example, if we were children of divorce or addiction, if we experienced too much protection or not enough discipline, affection, or financial stability, if we endured abuse of any kind, or if we lived through an illness or tragedy of our own or within the family, we probably became enmeshed in a personal opinion of powerlessness, victimhood, consciousness, or resentment of self or others that could have halted our ability to let go of early childhood small-mindedness and trust going further into a more expansive experience of life and ourselves.

No matter what occurred in our earlier days, by the time we were adolescents, our toolkit for adult thinking was going to be blended with eagerness, confidence, talents, desires, insecurities, hurts, and fears. This mixture became the ingredients of highs and lows during the adolescent stage. We pushed to be different while struggling to be approved and part of a team or peer group we decided had the best sense of belonging.

The adolescent stage was pivotal for the phase to follow, which would lead us into lifelong self-realization. All during adolescence, we bantered back and forth between comparisons and contrasts while we were learning to interact with others, hopefully more effectively. Very often, our unlearned or unresolved issues from earlier days got played out on the stage of our peers, teachers, coaches, and family members. High school could have been the place where we blindly vented our resentments or fears that were rooted in family dynamics like control and authority issues, sibling rivalry or birth order entitlement issues, new responsibilities and self-motivation issues, or uncertainty about the metaphors of our maturing bodies, both internally and externally, to state a few.

Adolescence was a stage of great, intense polarities, which were a combination of letting go to be freer and more prepared for adult life and the rigid fear of changing and stepping outside of our childhood comfort zones. We were never more dualistic than during this stage. This stage had great impact on our ability to let go and leave home a little behind in order to feel the effects of our own decision-making process. What was also important was trusting we could go home for support, advice, and comfort in order to recharge and try it all again.

The power of the polarities we may have experienced was, again, not because everything was perfect, but because through all of the dysfunctional, unpredictable twists and turns, we got to see deeper and deeper layers of ourselves. The real prize of the adolescent stage was the ability to begin to understand that "they" were not going to make or break who were to become. The prize was a newfound version of self that hopefully could begin to sift through childhood flaws and family imperfections in order to focus on becoming someone who felt good about being that particular kind of someone.

The more we could let go of the fear of what lay ahead and know with a certainty that we were loved and supported, the greater the feeling of personal victory at having weathered the storms of extremes so often scripted in this distinctive stage of life.

Regardless of how well we felt we might have fared through those years, the inner wisdom of our soul still remains the constant mentor and healer. Our inner holy presence never left us, nor will it ever leave us. Our holy presence is always there to rein in the polarities and tensions of our lives and simply waits for us to choose the peaceful inner guidance in any moment, even if we felt we didn't properly receive it during crucial earlier times.

Our soul is home to the holy presence waiting to comfort us so that we can correct what was or might have been. Within us, there is always the timeless choice and freedom to be more than before.

Remedy for learning and letting go:

* Sit quietly with your eyes closed.
* Create an easy rhythm for your breathing and allow all of your attention to be focused on the center of your chest, where you know your heart and soul to be.
* Sense a beautiful, gentle, golden light in the center of your chest that seems to radiate and increase with every inhalation and exhalation.
* Focus upon the pulsating golden light as you allow yourself to imagine your beautiful safe haven.
* Remain in your safe haven and create as much detail as desired. Feel as if you are really there.
* Remember, every time you are in your safe haven, the holy presence is always there waiting to guide, assist, and comfort you.
* Examine these questions with the holy presence and pause to reflect upon any insights or awareness.
  - What feeling, event, friend, trial, or triumph from your adolescence seems to stand out or immediately come to mind?
  - How did this memory shape you?
  - Did it have a positive or negative impact upon you?
  - Did you struggle with confidence during these years? Examples: relationships, sports, siblings, first love, sex experience, academics.
  - Did you feel you began to learn self-motivation, responsibility, and personal freedom during these years?
  - In what areas of your life did you feel most insecure or vulnerable, and are these still areas of concern now?
  - What hurt or frightened you most during these years?

- Were you ever in a situation of fear or danger, and how did you manage to get through it?
- Was there any significant event or loss that may have delayed or interrupted your development during your adolescence? Examples: loss of pet, a relocation, divorce, death of a loved one, illness in the family, trauma.
- What was the greatest victory or positive empowering experience that you can recall from your adolescence, and how has it affected your adult life?

* Ask the holy presence to grant you ample wisdom, insight, and new interpretations about your adolescence that can help you realize how resilient you really are, and how you can trust the process of life regardless of the situation now, past, present, and future.

* Take your time reflecting upon these insights. It is suggested that you record these reflections in a journal for further review.

Incline your ear and hear the words of the wise and apply your mind to my knowledge for it will be pleasant if you keep them within you, if all of them are ready upon your lips. That your trust may be in the Lord; I have made them known to you today, even to you.

—Proverbs 22:17–19

CHAPTER 5

Reloading to Launch

$\mathcal{A}$s the next learning phase of our lives was expanding before us, once again, we were met with a polarity of compelling emotions. Throughout the trials and triumphs of adolescence, we were perhaps introduced to the reality of how good and awful life can feel. Through those years, we accumulated a powerful file of great experiences ranging from the thrills of bonded friendships, romance, risky adventures, and immeasurable, yet markable, first-time encounters with our newly found freedom to the painful depths of rejection, loneliness, fear, and threat of failure. The major struggle during those years might have been just attempting to stay centered as the endless process of "who am I?" continued to unfold.

Regardless of what we claimed as success or failure, most important was the lesson of letting go. We had to adjust over and over again to what did work out for us and what didn't. Those years provided the necessary tools for transforming the intense duality of life into rich discernment, which would prepare us for further choice making in our adult lives. We needed to both fail and succeed in order to ascertain a refinement of identity that would continue to focus on our potential and not just what the resulting circumstances might have felt like.

As we were continuing to let go of unrealistic uncertainties and certainties, we moved into the next phase of life somewhere during the late teens and early twenties. During this learning curve, we felt a variety of emotions according to our evaluation of the prior stage.

During the late teens and early twenties, it became more and more apparent that we were on our way, like it or not, to being groomed for adulthood and its inherent independence, responsibilities, and accountabilities. We were swirling with "Look out, world, here I come!" and "Oh, no, I don't want to look at that big world." We had to learn how to get ready for the biggest jump into life in our lives at that time. We needed to learn how to assess where we had been and then constructively decide where we might go, but do this with much more personal input and accountability. The margin of error might have felt enormous, numbing, or exciting.

These years called for concise self-inventory, reevaluation, and exploration of infinite possibilities. These years, therefore, can be noted as the great initiating times for the "reloading to launch" phase. These years were marked by letting go of the designated circumstance of our lives in order to step into the world at large with the intent to truly be launched into a clearer and more purposeful sense of autonomy. Often this time is flooded with decisions about college and career paths.

We might have been overly enthusiastic about leaving home and venturing forth to college, new friends, and lots more freedom. We might also have been petrified by the fear of the unknown, being away from the comforts of home, not fitting in, academic failure, or appropriate decisions regarding alcohol, drugs, sex, and relationships. We may have made career and job choices without higher academic pursuits that also brought equal portions of certainty and uncertainty.

This "reloading to launch" phase was meant to highlight the power and impact of our choices. This phase could have frozen us in time for a while or propelled us into fast-forward personal evaluation and self-reliance. We were old enough to have some frame of reference about what we were drawn to and yet not sophisticated enough to realize how choices might ripple us forward in both favorable and unfavorable ways. We probably already had inclinations, desires, dreams, or expectations of both ourselves and outside influences that caused us to shape attitudes about what our lives could become, yet we may not have fully understood how to manifest these hopes, wishes, and dreams.

This time frame was filled with blended doubts and hopeful imaginings. There might have been a myriad of questions that for the first time we were having to answer for ourselves. Life was clearly getting us to leave the nest, and so we actually may have revisited some aspects of our very first exit out of the womb and into this earthly existence. As was mentioned earlier, the key lesson from the birth experience was leaving the "mystifying love" bond felt while in the womb, where all our needs were met with no effort on our part. We knew and felt unconditional love, and it was breathing through every cell of our developing new bodies. It was heaven breathing in us, and we felt safe and loved.

These feelings and their truth remained with us and will continue to do so at every phase of life, whether we are aware, willing, or not. In fact, at specific times in every phase of our life, these mystifying love feelings reignite within us as a reminder of a deeper meaning, value, and purpose for who we are and our infinite bond to the holy presence.

An example of this potent sparking of being wrapped in the safety feeling can perhaps be best exemplified in our first love relationship. Whoever it was and for however long it lasted, it felt like heaven. That first relationship created deep inner etchings about our integrity, sexuality, and capacity to be transformed by love itself. It made us become someone else, both during and after. That first love relationship inspired, healed, satisfied, and stretched us beyond what we could have predicted. In its early interactions, we were enmeshed in and consumed by the thoughts, feelings, and experiences of our first love. We were maybe even absorbed into the relationship as another world.

Through this relationship, we floated into the all-encompassing expressions of love. It was heaven. In truth, it was a rekindling of the feelings of unity in God's love that we had before we were born. It was love for the sake of loving when we were in the womb. Somewhere during our first love relationship, this experience resurfaced, even though at the time, we didn't fully understand its divine roots.

First love relationships were an integral part of the lessons to be learned during the reloading to launch phase. These profound and often turbulent relationships were meant to bring us to new landscapes about ourselves, both internally and externally. Externally, we literally did different things. We went new places, met new people, and explored a diversity that veered away from our family customs and routines. Internally, we took some risks and had to assess situations on our own. We were confronted with challenges about drugs, alcohol, sexuality, trust, and vulnerability. Throughout this first love relationship with all its ups and downs, we were still drawn to the feeling of unity and acceptance with this special person that we had not experienced in that way with anyone else before. It was the feeling of unity and acceptance in the first love relationship, which is a reflection of God's ever-present love for us, that made that relationship so memorable, more than the duration or outcome of the relationship itself.

That first love relationship also taught us to connect to our inner being, which might not have been available prior to the relationship. Even though we are eternally one with the holy presence, and we knew and felt this before our birth, awareness and access to the divine seems to fade as we become preoccupied with learning the ways of the world through grade school and high school years. Oftentimes, it's the first love relationship and/ or concerns about choices to be made during young adulthood that brings us the opportunity to find our way back to inner sense about life, worldly expectations, and our connections to and placement within them.

First love relationships and career choices set the stage for how we were to be in the world and ultimately trust the process of life itself. Through these experiences, we were meant to spark our own personal desires to love and be loved, as well as to feel the worthiness of following a purposeful path that would serve ourselves and not merely the dictates of the tribal mind or consensus consciousness.

Through this phase of reloading to launch, we were meant to explore lessons about approval versus disapproval within ourselves and others at a deeper level and begin to realign to the holy presence who always loves, guides, and protects us. As this phase unfolded, the hopeful intent was that we could establish the beginning of an inner dialogue with the holy presence that we felt was trustworthy. Even if we called the inner connection our "gut instinct," it would be sufficient to become a foundation pathway that we could build upon throughout the rest of our lives. During our late teens and into our young adulthood, there were opportunities that drew upon our inner feelings as a source of insight and wisdom, even if we were unaware at the time. As we made our decisions, they were based more upon inner self-reliance and support of others rather than the predominant inclinations and persuasions of others. During these years, trial and error was often the best mentor. Experience now included a deeper inner sense of self and a connection to the divine, who is always present to assist in the unfolding of who we were meant to be.

Somewhere during our late teens through our young adult years, we made decisions that proved the power of cause and effect once again. Those decisions launched us into a particular direction that may still, to this day, be affecting us in both positive and/or negative ways. In any case, we needed to get "launched."

Remedy for learning and letting go:

* Sit quietly with your eyes closed.
* Create an easy rhythm for your breathing and allow all of your attention to be focused on the center of your chest, where you know your heart and soul to be.
* Sense a beautiful, gentle, golden light in the center of your chest that seems to radiate and increase with every inhalation and exhalation.
* Focus upon the pulsating golden light as you allow yourself to imagine a beautiful place where you feel totally free, calm, and safe. This place may be real or imaginary. This place is your safe haven.
* Remain in your safe haven and create as much detail as desired. Feel as if you are really there.
* Remember, every time you are in your safe haven, the holy presence is always there waiting to guide, assist, and comfort you.
* Examine these questions with the holy presence and pause to reflect upon any insights or awareness.
  - Can you recall the feelings of your first love relationship and how it changed you at the time?
  - How did this relationship cause you to define love in positive and/or negative ways?
  - Did you feel resolved about this relationship, or is it still feeling unfair or incomplete?
  - How did this relationship pave the way for other relationships up until now?
  - Have you let go of the outdated definitions of love and self-worth?

- Are you focused more on how to love yourself than on seeking love/approval from others, both personally and professionally?
- How did your early choices about education and career impact where you are now?
- Do you have any regrets about choices you made during your late teens and young adult years? Examples: sex, pregnancy, drugs, alcohol, money issues, procrastination, work ethic, following inner guidance.
- Can you allow the holy presence to guide, direct, and heal these old perspectives and patterns so you can appreciate a new sense of self-worth and who you became through these choices?
- Was there a significant event during these years that may have delayed or interrupted your freedom of choice concerning your desires and dreams? Examples: divorce, loss of a loved one, financial issues, personal or family trauma or illness, relocation.
- Can you allow the holy presence to grant you the wisdom needed so you reevaluate the course of your life during these years and how it shaped you into a better version of yourself?

* Ask the holy presence to dissolve and heal any and all lingering regrets, shame, insecurities, blame, hurt, or guilt concerning choices made during your late teens and young adult years.

* Ask the holy presence to infuse you with a deeper sense of self-worth and a stronger connection to the inner guidance that is always available to you.

* Take your time reflecting upon these insights. It is suggested that you record these reflections in a journal for further review.

Trust in the Lord with all your heart and lean not on your own understanding; in all ways acknowledge Him and He will make your paths straight.

—Proverbs 3:5, 6

CHAPTER 6

Time to Be Me, Again

s the years and experiences kept accumulating, we probably became accustomed to the motion of the pendulum of our lives as learned from successes, failures, deeper love, broken hearts, family bonding, and family or societal criticism. We probably created a couple of dreams that did come true, like a relationship, business, career, home, vacation, or family of our own, which felt good and encouraged us to pursue even greater realizations of our potential. Life and its endless possibilities could have really become our own. We might have even adapted to the ultimate truth that the only script/formula for successful living is the one that we create ourselves.

A deep internal freedom, hopefully, was starting to expand its wings. Regardless of whether the relationship or marriage worked or not, or whether money management skills enabled us to handle a balance in our thirties, forties, etc., or not, what became more and more evident was the underlying theme throughout every decision that the quality of our life was, is, and always will be equal to what and how we set it up to be. We decided with awareness, support, or approval, or without them, whether our life was going to be all we could make it or whether we would be entrapped by the false belief in limitations in ourselves or from the societal consciousness, which is mostly stuck in victim or fear consciousness.

From our late twenties and for virtually the rest of our lives, we were and are at the helm of our own destiny. Our paths were never meant to be a life sentence, but rather an ongoing celebration of re-creation and reshaping of ourselves as we decide to revamp greater visions or keep to a preconceived script and merely make the best of it. For these reasons, this phase, which is ultimately the rest of our lives, can best be described as the "time to be me, again" stage.

As we established a foundation for ourselves, we might have felt finally grounded and free simultaneously so that we could continue to make decisions, both proactively and reactively, according to who we have become to this juncture point. We could have chosen to maintain the status quo or decided to follow the road less traveled into an extraordinary life of our own design.

The significance here during the "time to be me, again" open-ended phase is not whether we chose a path maintaining a specific standard of stability and satisfaction or a path of eccentricity. The real power during these years is that we could and can change the direction of our lives at any time. This ultimate truth might have escaped us for the most part.

Another relevant truth was and is that whether we chose to maintain our lives or consistently re-create our lives, the holy presence within everything that breathes has a curriculum of its own that will always give evidence and direction to the greater meaning and purpose of our existence. Sometimes this ultimate curriculum is called the *logos*, which in Greek translates to the divine ordering factor of everything that is. The logos within us is set to allow every experience to bring us the opportunity to love ourselves, others, and our Creator more fully. This is and always will be the ultimate curriculum. We were all created in the image and likeness of God. How we reclaim the realization and how long it takes us are always our ultimate choice.

The logos curriculum itself is flawless. Our awareness of it varies according to what phase of life we are experiencing. Every phase from birth forth carried in it a lifeline thread to God's wisdom and love with specific applications highlighted through each phase.

During our first phase, from birth to about two years of age, the gentle voice of the logos was there whispering, "I didn't leave you, even though this place doesn't feel like heaven." As a remedy, we were given the mystifying love experience of mother and other nurturing persons around us at that time. At our next phase, from three to six years old, the logos was moving us out into the world so we could begin the long process of individualization through school and its surrounding experiences. During these years, the holy presence was whispering, "You are unique. Go and learn how I created you as a one-of-a-kind child of God." As we grew through the next phase, somewhere between seven and ten, the Holy One was setting up a variety of situations that ranged from familiar and safe to thought-provoking and contrasting. These years invited us to begin to learn the many layers of the cause-and-effect duality that everyday circumstances can bring. Through this time, the logos was reminding us, "Even though there is so much that seems far beyond your grasp of understanding, I am always with you, keeping you safe." As the process continued through the next phase into adolescence, more challenges and contrasts ensued. Yet the Holy Logos was still always present within our inner being, explaining, "It's okay to go forward. Trust in My Presence. You were designed to be uniquely you." Even though there might have been some risky stepping stones, we all made it through to the next stage, including the bruises earned along the way. With a little experience, in fear of the unknown, we pushed through to the next stage of early adulthood. There may have been more uncertainties, fear of failure, loneliness, and the constant struggle for stability wavering between dependence and independence. Yet, the logos was always within us, speaking perhaps with signs and synchronistic events, saying, "Trust in Me. Feel your heart and trust it is Me guiding you. You are designed for a purpose even greater than what you know."

The perfection of the logos curriculum, however, is often not discovered until the later phase of adulthood, in the "time to be me, again" stage, which again is mostly the rest of our lives.

The perfection of the logos curriculum is revealed in an ongoing manner throughout our late twenties and forward with an accuracy that is not readily recognized. Regardless of the quality or our interpretation of success or failure throughout any prior phases due to loss, illness, family dysfunctionalities, addictions, trauma, tragedy, or unexpected blessings and breakthroughs, if any impact from any phase was missed, ignored, or unresolved, the logos curriculum will bring it back into our experience as many times as it takes until the lessons have been successfully learned and interpreted.

The unfinished lessons from birth to adulthood systematically appear as day-to-day events that can seem to be unwarranted conflicts. We believe these present-tense challenges could be irritating and unfair because we are analyzing them as if they are randomly occurring in the moment, when in fact these situations are actually best understood through the eyes of projection that is filtering through the current circumstances.

For example, if there was an unresolved or unfinished authority issue from the adolescent phase, these same issues could reappear with current employers or people in charge.

We might have changed jobs and career paths, but until the unresolved, erroneous control/victim patterns are purged, a similar personality conflict will repeat itself.

If there were unresolved issues during the birth and early childhood stage, there could be adult situations that, although they may feel like undesirable conflicts, were and are actually opportunities from the Holy Logos to heal, forgive, and set us free to flourish as the true safe child of God we were intended to be. Issues still needing to be reviewed and dissolved from these stages can show up in adult situations as codependent relationship struggles, fear of being alone, being overly responsible or irresponsible, motivation and depression issues, or inability to create a self-initiating life path.

These uncompleted, unhealed wounds would keep us unnecessarily dwarfed in our true potential and perpetuate useless pain. The Holy Logos curriculum allows the projection of these wounds to pop up in present daily experience so that we can correct the perception of why and how these false personal assessments occurred and, most importantly, so that the holy presence can erase the inappropriate thinking permanently. We needed the current painful situation to occur in order to remember its true rooted source so that it could be eradicated forever through petition to Spirit and its gracious unending response of "*Yes*, it is done."

Another example of the logos's flawless formula for the cause of our freedom and wholeness can stem from unresolved events from later childhood and into adolescence. Ongoing patterns of the need for approval or fixation with competition, winning, and self-image, as well as bodily appearance, selfishness, control/anger issues, and inability to follow through or complete tasks and ideas, can arise from damaged beginnings during these years. These reminiscent feelings will find their way into our relationships, career paths, money issues, and overall ability to allow ourselves to be confident and happy.

Whenever such feelings arise, most will ignore or hold to the opinion of being powerless to transform the situation effectively. Perhaps this can explain why many young adults have already dimmed their luster to the truth, the glorious adventure of creating a life filled with endless possibilities. The Holy Logos is the infinite wisdom and love that is God infinitely accessible to us. We need only to connect from within, review the conflict, and ask, and it is given. In truth, this is the shining delight of being an adult. We were meant to discern, remember, correct, and set it free.

During our young adult years, we may have been given opportunities to do this, but if we didn't have the faith tools to follow the healing formula, we may have been left with more disempowering victim attitudes. We did and will make mistakes or foster errors in judgment. This, too, is part of the journey. Letting go of flawed-premise thinking is what was meant to restore us to the unique signature of the divine as God created us. If we were not encouraged or taught a satisfying faith connection to our inner being, reclaiming our God-self can clearly be delayed.

Such delays could have happened through experiences with law officials, untimely pregnancies, accidents, loss of a beloved friend or family member, illness, broken relationships, financial frustration, or disasters caused by weather conditions. Without the faith connection to our inner being, we could have been left with a deep scar that reads, "Why did this happen?"

Adult years could be filled with *whys* and *what ifs*. As much as we were thrilled to finally be on our own, as years passed, it could easily be falsely perceived as a random soup of *maybes*, *whys*, and *oh noes*. We could easily fall prey to the commonplace illusions and the crippling fears funneled through the media, political banter, and their false authority conjectures, religious values, and their false control through skewed meanings of reward, guilt, and punishment.

It can feel like a daily struggle to find ourselves and a confident feeling of belonging. The Holy Logos is the inner connection to the absolute truth of God and our absolute safety in God. The power is, was, and always will be in Him, with Him, and through Him. We cannot and will not ever be separated from the Creator. We were created by the Source and eternally tethered, no matter what we falsely experienced, believed, or were taught. The Holy Logos is the great and divine corrector and can peel away all false notions acquired since birth and throughout the rest of our lives. Through a repetitive, even daily, connection with our inner being through prayer, meditation, and reflection, we can be returned to our true safe haven in a matter of moments. Falsehoods, wounds, a false sense of self, and powerlessness can fade away daily, leaving only our true self connected to God in peace, joy, and love. This is the true adventure of adulthood with all its ups and downs, proving once again the power of logos and its lesson—let go and become more than before.

Remedy for learning and letting go:

* Sit quietly with your eyes closed.
* Create an easy rhythm for your breathing and allow all of your attention to be focused on the center of your chest, where you know your heart and soul to be.
* Sense a beautiful, gentle, golden light in the center of your chest that seems to radiate and increase with every inhalation and exhalation.
* Focus upon the pulsating golden light as you allow yourself to imagine a beautiful place where you feel totally free, calm, and safe. This place may be real or imaginary. This place is your safe haven.
* Remain in your safe haven and create as much detail as desired. Feel as if you are really there.
* Remember, every time you are in your safe haven, the holy presence is always there waiting to guide, assist, and comfort you.
* Examine the following concerns or issues and pause to reflect upon any insights or awareness.
  - Is there a reoccurring pattern in your present life that you are willing to see differently now in order that it may be resolved? Examples: anger, sadness, self-resentment or loathing, lack of motivation, feeling unloved or unappreciated, feelings of insecurity or fear about the future, confusion or wounds about sexuality, feelings of isolation or not fitting in, fears, angers, confusion about God, abandonment, disappointment, unfulfilled dreams.
  - Allow yourself to be drawn to a specific emotion that seems to be magnified at this time.

- Remain focused upon the light of the holy presence and declare to the logos, "I am ready and willing to see the truth and purpose of this issue."
- Relax and breathe; take your time.
- Ask the logos to show you the book of your life, which may be a large photo album.
- Ask the logos to go back to a specific set of circumstances that will help you understand the source of why and how you feel the way you do now.
- Ask the logos to illuminate the photos from your book of life that will best assist you in understanding the impact of this situation upon your adult life.
- Ask to see why it occurred as it did and the soul lesson that you were designed to achieve.
- Ask to see the ripple effect it has had upon you over the course of your life.
- Ask to be shown the divine purpose in this issue and the blessings to you that may still be waiting to be released from within you once your perception changes.
- Ask for the insight, love, and grace to forgive everything from everyone, including yourself.
- Ask for the forgiveness to be permanent and inclusive of any and all residual negative effects within you and any aspect of your life, physically, financially, and spiritually.
- Ask for increase of divine light for the rest of your life in all you do, say, think, and feel.
- Relax and be willing to receive this healing light.
- Be thankful and accept it as done in the name of the Most High God, who deeply loves you.

* Take your time reflecting upon these insights. It is suggested that this process be repeated as often as you feel necessary. It is suggested that you record these reflections in a journal for further review.

Do not conform any longer to the pattern of the world, but be transformed by the renewing of your mind. Then you will be able to prove what God's will is; His good, pleasing and perfect will.

—Romans 12:2

PART TWO

Heavenly Returns

CHAPTER 7

Me Without You

The first sting of death knows no age, nor season, and probably pierced our hearts regardless of our ability to understand at the moment of the loss itself.

My first experience of someone dying who was close to me was the death of my maternal great-grandmother, Rosaria. She was a significant matriarch in our family. She gave birth to sixteen children, nine of whom lived full-term lives. Although she could not read or write in English, she managed to secure her own savings account by renting empty garages across the street from her home and without my great-grandfather's knowledge. She financed her sons to start a construction business by purchasing a truck and shovels. This simple beginning blossomed into a multimillion dollar company that lasted for three generations. Upon her death, there was a surprising amount of money still liquid in her account, which totally shocked my great-grandfather Salvatore.

My great-grandmother was called Grandma, and her eldest daughter, my maternal grandmother, was known as Nana Mary. I loved my early childhood. We lived in Newark, New Jersey, in a two-family house owned by my paternal grandparents, Papa Migo and Nana Angelina. They lived downstairs, and we lived upstairs. My maternal grandparents, Papa Larry and Nana Mary, lived across the street. Our street was lined with aunts, uncles, and cousins, and our great-grandparents were only on the next block. Our doors were never locked, and relatives were always present as part of our daily events, along with the endless availability of savory delights of "leftovers," homemade cookies, and espresso. For me, it was truly a heavenly way to begin my life's journey.

Then, one day, that heavenly feeling got jolted. I was five years old and, as usual, in the kitchen with both grandmothers and my mother. The phone rang, and an icy stare came over my mother's face as she looked to us and softly muttered, "Grandma just died." That moment of silence felt like an eternity. Then, without instruction, we were all huddled together in an endless embrace that was washed by the mixture of everyone's tears. I clearly remember feeling, "Something's not good!" Yet, feeling everyone's hugging arms, I still felt safe.

Very often, I will reflect through my prayers and meditations upon that time when Grandma died. I think about her brilliance and resilience as an uneducated immigrant. I think about what she brought to the generations after her. And I think about how she taught me the ultimate paradox about death, even though I was definitely too young to grasp the lesson of her death at the time. Decades and many experiences of death later, I realized the power of that long embrace that included four generations the day Grandma died. Death, although a loved one seems separated from us, invites us to feel a deeper love among us.

At the moment any death occurs, we are confronted with a depth of emotions that may not have any words or explanations at the time. We can feel like we've been thrust into a blank abyss of the unknown. Our minds and thoughts can rush and race for logical steps to get out of the painful void, while no sense of rationality offers immediate comfort. We may just be numb and almost empty of any plausible direction. Some of us will rise up through prayer, faith, and purpose to function for loved ones around us. Yet others may lash out at God as the only semblance of prayer available.

Just as each life has its own signature journey, so does each person's death. Regardless of when we experienced our first loss, our life's path was altered, even if we were too young or simply unaware of the impact at the time. No matter what was the cause or the nature of the relationship between the person who died and ourselves, we became a different person through the experience.

Very often, however, we were not able to ascertain who we became through the loss of our loved one until a much later time. It is only and always a matter of time for us that we will wake up to the deep inner truth of every experience, both in life and through death of a loved one. Change is the natural, inevitable, and greatest teacher. Letting go is hard and mostly painful.

In order for us to appreciate the pain both of loss and of letting go, it can be helpful to reflect upon the actual psychological steps we might have experienced when our first loss of a loved one occurred. For these purposes, we will review the grief cycle as described by Elisabeth Kübler Ross. She identifies the process as a five-step cycle that moves us from the death or trauma into another evolutionary development of ourselves.

Upon the impact of the death itself, we typically experience step one, denial. We were in shock. Regardless of whether the announcement of the death was sudden or expected, our physical, emotional, mental, and spiritual systems can seemingly get jammed and come to a screeching halt, as if our whole being is shouting "Oh, no!" Denial, although sometimes subtle, seems to set in. Denial is a built-in mechanism that is a safeguard. It prevents us from dealing with our loss all at once. This could be referred to as a numb stage. Denial can take on a variety of forms. We might have retreated or rejected others. We might have tried to stay overly busy as a way of managing the pain of loss.

Eventually, time and the nature of the process move us to the next stage, anger. Anger is the emotional response to the loss that is deeply rooted in our fear of loss of control. Anger can take on many forms also. Our anger might have been known, hidden, blind, or denied. In any case, anger might have been a very difficult step that, for some, might have been almost impossible to move through. Who would not be angry as a result of the death of a child or a tragic accidental death of a spouse or family member? In this step, the anger may initially be natural, yet how long we remained at this step might have proven to be unhealthy.

Step three, bargaining, was our attempt to rationalize any and all *coulds*, *shoulds*, and *woulds*. This was our way of trying to "fix it" and a feeble way of feeling back in control again. This was our way of getting out all the emotional instability by using more logical sequencing in order to feel more grounded.

Again, the process and time moved us forward into the next stage, depression. This is where we have decided it probably is a hopeless situation and felt there were no solutions. We might have felt life could never get better. Sometimes, we might have even slipped into the dark night of the soul and experienced despair, loss of sleep or appetite, and loss of basic interest in any daily activities of life. How long we stayed at this stage varied with each individual's personality.

However, just as certain as the dark of night ushers in the dawn, we were invited into the final step of the grief cycle, acceptance. At this step, we recognized our upset about what happened, still perhaps wishing it was different, yet willing to go forward. We might have found a renewed faith, trust in other loved ones, strength, or a renewed purpose for our journey. Acceptance takes time. We might not have had the availability of time at the moment of the loss of our loved one due to surrounding circumstances. Acceptance of our first loss might have occurred years later as a response to another death in present time, when we were more equipped emotionally, mentally or spiritually.

No matter what the case might have been, none of these stages are inherently negative or predictable, yet each stage is a necessity. We could never have been moved from denial to acceptance without the stages in the middle, regardless of the time it might have taken. The ultimate goal was to be gentle with ourselves and move through the process in order to reclaim the timeless truth. Death is not final, a failure, or a punishment, no matter how or when it occurs. For the loved one who died, it is a glorious homecoming to other deceased loved ones and the eternal, magnanimous love God has for us. For us who were left behind, it is the endless invitation to let go of false-premise thinking and responses to life's conditions and begin to feel the experience of eternal love now, while still in our earthly bodies, by allowing the loss to teach us how to let go from the depths of emotions that could have outwardly altered how we live. If we let ourselves trust our deceased loved ones to help in the process of healing, the void between heaven and earth may not feel so vast. Heavenly help is always available.

Healing, living, loving, losing are and always will be an ongoing process. Our first experience of losing someone may have occurred during our earlier years while we were ourselves in the midst of our developmental stages. If someone died before we were in our adult years, the five stages of the grief cycle would have become interwoven with the age-appropriate "letting go" lessons that were explained in earlier chapters. Therefore, the result of the loss may have created a type of arrested development due to the interruption of growth caused by the death and the subsequent life changes that occurred. In any event, it is important to remember that the Holy Logos of our inner being is divine wisdom and divine love. The Holy Logos always sets forward the proper curriculum for our soul's highest purposes. The Holy Logos is our sacred navigation system with one purpose, and one purpose only: that we would reclaim our true identity of being made in the image and likeness of God and reclaim His love that is always within us.

Certainly, this truth seems difficult to comprehend, trust, and integrate into our daily lives, yet it is, was, and always will be the truth. We came from love and were made by love to share love eternally, past, present, and forever. Our first experience with death shakes our finite existence to its core at any age. This is its hidden blessing. As we experience our first "me without you," whether we are aware of it or not, we are pushed forward into a great remembrance of who we really are. The power of our first experience with the death of a loved one is the glorious invitation to help us let go of limited thinking proposed by the finite world and set us free into the infinite life that is always available for those who seek it and choose it. The power of the first loss of a loved one is the gift to help us live in more eternal love now without dying in order to understand it. Our first loss and its ripple effects probably could take a lifetime to grasp and appreciate.

May we remain blessed by all those who have gone before us.

Remedy for learning and letting go:

* Sit quietly with your eyes closed.
* Create an easy rhythm for your breathing and allow all of your attention to be focused on the center of your chest, where you know your heart and soul to be.
* Sense a beautiful, gentle, golden light in the center of your chest that seems to radiate and increase with every inhalation and exhalation.
* Focus upon the pulsating golden light as you allow yourself to imagine a beautiful place where you feel totally free, calm, and safe. This place may be real or imaginary. This place is your safe haven.
* Remain in your safe haven and create as much detail as desired. Feel as if you are really there.
* Remember, every time you are in your safe haven, the holy presence is always there waiting to guide, assist, and comfort you.
* Examine the following events, concerns, and issues, and pause to reflect upon any insights or awareness.
  - Who was the first person who died that was of a significant relationship?
  - How old were you and in what stage of development were you at the time?
  - Allow yourself to remember and reflect upon this first loss of a loved one, and be sure to ask the holy presence for assistance and clarity.
  - How did this first death experience influence your life, family, and decisions at the time?
  - Do you remember your own personal and emotional responses to this loss and how it altered your thinking, behavior, and decisions?

- Were you too young to process the impact of this death? If so, when did you address its influence in your life and development?
- Do you ever dream of this loved one? Or pray or seek to speak with him or her?
- Know that your loved one is still connected to you and always available. Ask the holy presence to connect you to your loved one. You may discuss anything with him or her, past, present, and to come.

* It is suggested that you write down your questions before speaking with your loved one. Then while in your safe haven, ask the holy presence to direct you into a peaceful connection with your deceased loved one. Ask your questions one at a time, slowly, to assure clarity.

* Ask the holy presence to also help you to understand any unresolved lessons or issues between you and your deceased loved one. Be willing to let go of any preconceived ideas and feelings so you can become aware of the divine truth and love needed to help this relationship heal completely. Be willing to let go and let the holy presence bless and heal both of you into a new, loving connection and relationship.

* Know that you can repeat this meditation process as often as desired.

* Take your time reflecting upon these insights. It is suggested that as you review the prayerful process, you record these reflections in a journal for further reference.

Let not your hearts be troubled; believe in God, believe also in me. In my Father's house there are many rooms; if it were not so, would I have told you that I go to prepare a place for you? And when I go and prepare a place for you, I will come again and will take you to myself, that where I am you may be also. And you know the way where I am going.

—John 14:1–4

CHAPTER 8

Rebirthing Me Without You

Whenever we experience death, regardless of whether it is the lingering effects of our first significant loss, other deceased loved ones, or even hearing of a death that occurred in our surrounding environment, such as prominent societal figures or through violent outbursts and casualties, we feel affected.

Death moves us, changes us even to the cellular level of our bodies. We feel its pain, void, and often injustice to the depths of our beings. These emotions, although sometimes unidentifiable, are not inherently negative. Even though the indescribable pain may have seemed to permeate our entire being with such finality, the blessed paradox in both life and death will prevail. Change is the only constant, and its law is and always will be throughout all aspects of life and death.

As certain as day is after night, so too were we to move on, live on after the loss of a loved one. Even if we experienced the death of a loved one early on in life and were not able to fully process its impact on our lives, we were thrust forward, as if on fast forward, into an unfamiliar life path that might have made us feel like we were living without a script, plan, purpose, or sense of security—or sanity, for that matter.

We had to live without on many levels. We had to live without, of course, the physical presence of our loved one, which in and of itself can feel unexplainable and at times unbearable. We may have shouted out aloud, alone or with others, "Where did he/she go? I can't feel him/her, touch him/her anymore!" This layer of living without can feel the most painful. There were, however, other aspects to process through as well.

We had to learn to live in different daily routines. Meal time, sleep time, phone conversation routines, holidays, and traditions all seemed to change abruptly, with no known or familiar remedy immediately available. Every aspect of our lives shifted when our loved one left.

The empty space that once was theirs probably felt like a bottomless pit. Somewhere in a long, silent moment, we might have acknowledged our lives would never be the same. Somewhere in that moment, the Holy Logos was right there, gently inviting us to step forward in new ways, slowly and one step at a time, into a different understanding about life, death, and ourselves. This invitation was and is ever-present, without an expiration date, and it only needs the quiet response from us from within our hearts, "Okay, show me, and help me go forward."

With even the slightest gesture from our hearts, the holy presence would begin to use our tears to wash our souls so that a new vision and path could be revealed. Wherever there was a loss, the holy presence waited patiently to lift us into a new beginning that would always promise our loved ones, although no longer visible or touchable, were and still are always available. This defies the finite, three-dimensional version of life, yet it is the total truth nonetheless.

The wisdom bridge between this earthly existence and eternal life and between living with our loved ones and living without them begins with a tiny glimmer of faith. The Holy Logos uses this opening to prove that just as our deceased loved one's path has changed, so must ours. The more we can use the empty silence in a prayerful way, the more the Holy Logos will, in fact, show us and help us.

The eternal love and truth of God from within, although always waiting and available, never compels or impels us in any way. The Spirit of God is and always will be unconditional. So it is up to us, whenever we are ready, to embrace the power, comfort, and healing in the knowledge that death is never final, a failure, or a punishment for them or us, no matter what.

The truth of life and death is so much greater than our perceptions. All our perceptions are basically rooted in some form of fear or limitation. These premises are grossly incomplete and inaccurate. We can remain under these false impressions for a lifetime, since free will is also always operant. We can freely choose to stay in our false premise thinking or freely choose to step into truth, wisdom, peace, healing, comfort, and eternal life at any time. It only takes the smallest act of will through even the unspoken "show me and help me," and an entirely new way of living, loving, and being is revealed step by step.

Death gives the gift of accelerated evolution to both the deceased loved one and ourselves. For the deceased, they are instantly released from the limitations of their bodies and circumstances. They are freed into their original creation blueprint of love, joy, and wisdom. If we accept the invitation to follow the inner guidance from the Holy One from within, we too can become freed from false thinking and fearful thoughts about our own life and death. We can be shown and helped to the truth, that even though our deceased loved ones are no longer visible, they are ever-present through the endless channels of boundless love.

This is not a sentimental statement with a soothing intent. It is a scientific law, explained through quantum physics through a major principle of the universe. Simply stated, "Energy can neither be created nor destroyed, only transformed."

This law translates to our experience of life, as we are always in a constant phase of transformation. Death is a transformation that can bridge the seen and the unseen if we would just freely choose to allow the Divine Creator to show us and help us. With the acceptance of change and the comforting trust in God, we can transform our experience of life into a more meaningful one than we could have ever imagined possible.

As we allow a new life path to emerge as the result of the loss of a loved one, by no means is this to imply "Out of sight, out of mind." It is, in fact, just the opposite. If we would slowly allow our new path for life to emerge and also allow the spirit of and love of our deceased one to accompany us through the process, we would begin to feel the permanent linkage between this world and the next, and our present life transformation would feel more grounded, safe, and fortifying.

As our new path emerges, we may experience new routines, locations, and relationships, and a new faith experience as well. Some of the habits and customs we used to engage in may be gone, but the value of those experiences is permanently inscribed upon our hearts. The value of every person, place, adventure, hurt, or healing has served to reshape us into a greater version of ourselves, and this reality becomes magnified through the death of our loved one and the subsequent changes in our lives that might have occurred.

Death changes everything and everyone involved. Although its painful void can linger, by the plan of the Holy Logos we can be filled with a deeper sense of our love for the deceased one, as well as a deeper gratitude for those who are still with us. Death is the greatest teacher about love, forgiveness, and transformation into becoming more than before, if we would only whisper from our grieving hearts, "Show me and help me." Then, in that whisper, new worlds would be revealed, and we would feel truth, peace, love, and eternal life emerge.

Remedy for learning and letting go:

* Sit quietly with your eyes closed.
* Create an easy rhythm for your breathing and allow all of your attention to be focused on the center of your chest, where you know your heart and soul to be.
* Sense a beautiful, gentle, golden light in the center of your chest that seems to radiate and increase with every inhalation and exhalation.
* Focus upon the pulsating golden light as you allow yourself to imagine a beautiful place where you feel totally free, calm, and safe. This place may be real or imaginary. This place is your safe haven.
* Remain in your safe haven and create as much detail as desired. Feel as if you are really there.
* Remember, every time you are in your safe haven, the holy presence is always there waiting to guide, assist, and comfort you.
* Examine the following concerns and issues, and pause to reflect upon any insights or awareness.
  - Are you ready and willing to see the before, during, and after your loved one's death through the eyes of Spirit and not just from your human perspective?
  - Are you ready and willing to ask for the holy presence to guide you to a broader understanding?
  - Are you ready and willing to say to the holy presence, "Show me and help me"?

* Are you willing to spend fifteen to thirty minutes daily so you can hear the Spirit's truth concerning the death of your loved one?

* Write down any and all questions you might have concerning the before, during, and after the passing of your loved one and how it may have impacted your life.
* Ask one question at a time while in your safe haven. Trust your first impressions and write them down in a journal.
* Then ask the following questions one at a time. Trust your first impressions and write them down in your journal.
  - Where do I belong now?
  - What do I need to let go of physically, emotionally, financially, mentally, or spiritually?
  - What do I need to do to start over and rebuild my life?
  - How can my deceased loved one still help me?
  - How can I trust that my deceased loved one is safe and in God's love?
  - How can I trust my life will be safe and provided for?
  - Does my deceased loved one hear me, feel me?
  - How can I ask for a sign that will prove to me that my deceased loved one is always with me?
  - How can I let go enough so I can feel peace, joy, comfort, and love again?

* Take your time reflecting upon these insights. It is suggested, of course, that you record these reflections in a journal for further review.

I will lead the blind by ways they have not known along unfamiliar paths. I will guide them; I will turn the darkness into light then and make the rough places smooth. These are the things I will do; I will not forsake them, says the Lord.

—Isaiah 42:16

CHAPTER 9

Where Are They Now?

Regardless of where we are in the grief process, time and life always continue to move us forward. Even though the death of our loved one can make it feel like our own life has come to a screeching halt, time does pass, seasons do change, and so do we. As we allow the grief process to carry us along, there is so much we can learn. And again, the key to the living and dying ongoing phases of life remains the same. We need to let go of what was in order to become even greater than before.

This is true for our deceased loved ones also. Life is eternal. We are eternal. They are eternal. Love is eternal. What changes is the form in which we lived and loved. This is true for the living and those who have moved on. What is difficult to grasp is where they are now. We can't see them or touch them as we did before, so sometimes the void keeps us in a false confinement of unknowingness. Since our emotions can often keep us in the illusory prison of fear of the unknown, science can create an open door for a greater quality of loving and communicating with our dearly departed.

The foundational principle of all life is energy. Energy is vibration of the life force that can be observed and measured through our advanced forms of technology that weren't previously available. We are essential vibrational energy, both seen and unseen. For example, we can see our physical bodies, yet not our emotions, our thoughts, or the spirit of God within us, even though they all exist simultaneously.

As the continuum of life moves us forward, that which we no longer need disappears so we can evolve into a greater version of self. This becomes particularly evident whenever we focus and reflect upon old photos of ourselves. We are no longer that person, in that body, feeling those emotions and thinking those thoughts. We have changed and evolved many times over while remaining who we are. Who we were can still be felt, while who we are now takes precedence.

We are all in the same constant evolutionary process of becoming a greater version of ourselves according to our choices and willingness to let go of fear. Fear, at its core, is a low vibration of energy that makes us feel limited and powerless. It is always a false notion because its opposite, which is all-powerful and all-knowing love, always resides within us. Love is the highest vibration of life. Love is the frequency of God expressing itself through us. We are invited to evolve out of fear and into love with every choice we make. Each choice, therefore, is a creation experience of either fear or love. Our choices keep moving us into greater fear and limitation or greater love and freedom. If our choices move us more consistently into love and freedom, we experience life as God truly intended. Our life can be quite a journey of heavenly adventures. Even the obstacles can still reveal God's love and miracles if we are willing to see each juncture through the eyes of the Holy Logos, who is ultimate love and freedom.

In death, regardless of the sum total of our choices, truth and love are revealed and experienced. We are no longer trapped in the fear consciousness of a conflicted mind or a confined body.

We see, feel, and become truth and love. In death, it is God's eternal love and truth that sets us free. We live on in an ongoing truth, love, and freedom environment. It is an environment that only vibrates with truth, love, and freedom. In death, we are returned to the original creation given by God. We are released into our original creation blueprint of being made in the image and likeness of God. Death creates a quantum leap for our personal evolution as we leave behind fear, limitation, and all false, painful illusions and entrapments. Death opens the doors to the infinite field of infinite possibilities because God's love is finally experienced for what it is—*real* and *eternal.*

Our deceased loved ones, having been welcomed into the endless dimension of truth and love, are eager to share the good news. They are eager to help us have our own leap of evolution through the true purpose of forgiveness. They are living in an environment that is without fear and pain, and they have quickly learned a deep and eternal truth. Fear caused pain, and forgiveness returns us to peace. If we were to examine our own earthly lives, we would find evidence of these eternal truths. Whenever we are trapped in fears, we feel the pain that our conflicted minds create. We worry about all that we could possibly imagine might go wrong. We see only our own powerlessness and the illusory scenarios that could manifest.

In those moments, we have lost sight of God, perhaps, and certainly of the presence of His love and wisdom, which is always within us. No matter; the situation we feared does get resolved, and our peace and calm can resurface again. During other times in our lives, we are feeling so relaxed, fulfilled, and loving. Maybe we are enjoying family, a vacation, or a celebration. We feel our inner being so light and free. Our thoughts are clear and nonjudgmental. We feel loved and maybe even inspired. These are the vibrations of God, heaven, and eternal love freely expressed. These are the experiences of our deceased loved ones because they see the truth of God without the distortion created by our earthly misinterpretations, false education, and false-premise thinking. Our deceased ones experience ongoing living, loving, and learning without fear. Their vibration is of love and truth, and they are always eager to share the good news if we allow them to do so.

With these truths in mind, some may ask, "But where are they, and why can't I see them?" The truthful answer is that they are with us and we can experience them, even though that seems so difficult to grasp.

If we let science and quantum physics guide us, we may be able to elevate our understanding of these truths. It has already been stated, but is worth repeating, that all life is energy. Energy can neither be destroyed nor created, only transformed. All life is energy vibrating at various rates of speed according to the quality of the frequency. The lower the frequency of energy is, the more fear-based it is. The higher the frequency of the energy is, the more love-based it is.

A useful visual as a helpmate to explain where we are and where our deceased ones are may be depicted in an analogy of a propeller on an airplane. When the airplane engine is not on or is running very, very slowly while still on the ground, we can see the individual propeller blades. When the engine is in high gear before, during, and after takeoff, the individual propeller blades are moving so fast we can't see them, even though they are still there.

While we are "on the ground" and in our bodies, our energies are like the propeller blades barely moving so we can see them. In death, our loved ones' energies become pure spirit and, as with the rapid-speed propeller blades, it becomes difficult to see them with our earthly eyes, even though they are really still there. Our departed ones are in light bodies, literally, and so are everything and everyone else with them. Sometimes this is referred to as multidimensional levels of coexisting dimensions. Perhaps a simpler way of expressing this is to say that heaven and earth are one.

If we would allow our loved ones to help us see what they see, they would. The prerequisite, however, is our willingness to let go of fear. This is necessary because of the fact that fear is always a lower frequency and inherently will not enable us to experience their high frequency of love dimension.

The abyss between what we can see or feel and that which appears to be unattainable is not without remedy. The bridge between the seen and unseen is always within us. God is within and everywhere, all the time. Forgiveness is the key that opens the ability to see, feel, and know what God sees, feels, and knows all the time, here, there, and everywhere. Forgiveness is the gift we give ourselves so we can enjoy our divine inheritance, here, there, and everywhere. Forgiveness can begin by going within to the heavenly oasis place where God is and asking to be shown a truthful and more loving perspective about an experience that might have caused us pain or hurt. As well as allowing our inner being to teach us a higher purpose for a negative experience, we will be allowing the frequency of who we are to transform into a higher frequency, moving out of fear-based thinking and into more love-based thinking. This transformation is truly life altering. This transformation is exactly the same kind of consciousness shifting that occurs with our deceased loved ones, except that they experience it in a much deeper, multifaceted, all-encompassing way. Sometimes this all-encompassing transformation is referred to as the life review or judgment day. A more precise explanation is that through death, our loved ones become more light, see more light, become more love, and release everything that is not. Forgiveness, both on earth and in heaven, releases everything in everyone that love is not.

It is this divine release that enables us to bring heaven to earth, in ourselves and even with our dearly departed. Letting go simply brings all love closer.

Remedy for learning and letting go:

* Sit quietly with your eyes closed.
* Create an easy rhythm for your breathing and allow all of your attention to be focused on the center of your chest, where you know your heart and soul to be.
* Sense a beautiful, gentle, golden light in the center of your chest that seems to radiate and increase with every inhalation and exhalation.
* Focus upon the pulsating golden light as you allow yourself to imagine a beautiful place where you feel totally free, calm, and safe. This place may be real or imaginary. This place is your safe haven.
* Remain in your safe haven and create as much detail as desired. Feel as if you are really there.
* Remember, every time you are in your safe haven, the holy presence is always there waiting to guide, assist, and comfort you.
* Examine the following concerns and issues, and pause to reflect upon any insights or awareness.
  - As you are relaxing and feeling calm in your safe haven with the holy presence, ask that you would be infused with more light throughout your entire energetic system. Ask the light to transmute to transcend all aspects of your complete multidimensional energetic being, including physically, emotionally, mentally, and spiritually. Ask for an increase of light with a gentle integration throughout all layers of your being.
  - Continue to breathe and relax through this cleansing and healing of self.

- Ask the holy presence to raise your frequency to become more love and less fear throughout the process.
- Then ask the holy presence to surround you in a safe light of celestial angels that can lift you to a sacred meeting place where you and a deceased loved one can meet.
- Relax and allow yourself to sense the sacred meeting place for you and the deceased loved one. Allow time as you continue to breathe and relax so you can experience as much detail as possible.
- Then, when you sense your loved one, allow yourselves to embrace one another so you can feel the love and light in a deep, calm, and peaceful way.
- Then proceed to ask any questions you choose. It may be helpful to write the questions down in your journal beforehand.
- For example, you may want to ask, "What are you doing now? Do you hear me, see me? Who's with you? Do you see God, Jesus, Mary? Are you healed? What did you learn about your earthly life after you died? Can you help me to trust in eternal life, love, and God? What do I need to let go of? Can you give me signs of your presence?"

* Take your time reflecting upon these insights. It is suggested that this process be repeated as often as you feel necessary. It is suggested that you record these reflections in your journal for further review.

And I saw the holy city, new Jerusalem, coming down out of heaven from God, prepared as a bride adorned for her husband; and I heard a loud voice from the throne saying, "Behold, the dwelling of God is with men. He will dwell with them, and they shall be His people, and God himself will be with them; he will wipe away every tear from their eyes and death shall be no more, neither shall there be mourning nor crying nor pain any more for the former things have passed away." And he who sat upon the throne said, "Behold I make all things new. Write this for these words are trustworthy and true. It is done! I am the alpha and the omega, the beginning and the end. To the thirsty I will give from the fountain of the water of life without payment. He who conquers shall have this heritage and I will be his God and he shall remain my child."

—Revelation 21:2–7

CHAPTER 10

Death Has No Sting!

No matter how many times we come face-to-face with losing someone or something, or have to confront a near-death experience for others or ourselves, or have felt the deep pain of the death of a relationship through divorce or betrayal, the core of these events and issues rattles us to the pit of our souls.

No matter what the cause, the effect, with or without awareness, subconsciously and/or consciously, can feel like a rejection, separation, or abandonment that may never heal. It can both define and confine the meaning, value, and purpose of our lives for the rest of our lives. It can close us off to our own undiscovered gifts and shut us down from the healing of divine love that we desperately need. For some, these life-altering experiences can be the catalyst to a greater quality of life than ever thought possible, once they have sufficiently lamented, processed, and perhaps forgiven themselves and others for a variety of reasons. They chose to make sense of it and reclaim a new version of self. They did not deny or avoid all the tender emotions that surfaced. They chose to find the sacred place within themselves and let the holy presence, through the path of the Holy Logos, show them the part of themselves that cannot and will not ever be torn, tarnish, or die. They allowed the holy, unending light of God breathing within them to find them, embrace, heal, and redirect them into a greater sense of living, loving everything and everyone. They made a choice not to let any experience diminish, destroy, or extinguish the divine inheritance to have eternal life and have it abundantly now. They decided to learn from the experience and not to let the experience control them.

Death and love are the greatest teachers. Both have a common denominator. Death and love can bring us to the depths of who we thought we were and invite us in to become more. Death and love can cause the greatest letting go of what was and, whether we are prepared or not, transform absolutely every aspect of the landscape of our present selves and life experiences. Death and love, both as individual experiences and simultaneous experiences, can allow the face of God to be made visible in ourselves and others.

Death and love are the greatest teachers for letting go of all finite perceived notions about safety and security and can cause us to remember the greatest truth, that God is always present within and around us, regardless of the perceived conditions, and His love and wisdom are always available to guide us into a greater life without end. His presence within and around us is His promise for our divine birthright, which is immortality.

Ultimately, every experience from our birth to our earthly death has the same lesson threaded throughout the span of earthly life. Every event, issue, circumstance, loss, hurt, rejection, betrayal, and abandonment is meant to help us remember the greatest gift by posing the same doubt, question, or fear. Every experience positions into the following inquiries. How did this event, person, place, or thing cause me to temporarily forget the presence and infinite power of God within me? How did

I seemingly lose myself, my power, or my infinite connection to God through these events? How did I allow myself to get temporarily trapped, confined, or limited due to outside conditions instead of remembering the endless, unconditional divine love within me? Every stage and phase throughout our lifespan will eventually bring us to these questions. If we allow it, by choice, we will always be guided into the all-encompassing love and healing that are God within us, so that we remember and truly feel safe and secure in just being ourselves anywhere, anytime, regardless of the situation.

Death and love became the constant fulcrum necessary to get us out of the false perceptions of feeling separate from God or abandoned by God and the subsequent illusory emotions of being powerless as a result. As we choose to go within to our inner being, even if it is only out of despair and desperation, the holy presence always wakes us back up to the eternal truth that we are loved, safe, and immortal. Through a steadfast journey within, we can remember and reclaim our infinite power by allowing the divine embrace to soothe and remind us who we really are, in Him, with Him, and through Him. No outside conditions, no matter what, can ever be greater than the power of God's unconditional and almighty truth and love that are eternally within us.

In this great remembrance, we are set free. No earthly experience, regardless of how grave it may be, can ever extinguish the eternal light and love that are God within us. We remember our eternal safety, and then even death has no power over us. We are instead ever-changing and immortally safe and loved. Death has no sting. Only love remains as the constant companion, teacher, healer, and reminder of who we really are in Him, with Him, and through Him, and so are all our beloved ones, here, there, and everywhere.

The pendulum of feeling powerless to powerful again in our divine nature is the purpose of all experiences throughout our earthly path. Every phase and stage is designed to give us the opportunity to remember our greatness through God's greatness within us. Every trial and triumph is meant to sharpen our awareness and focus so we can readjust our perspective about what is really valuable and important in life.

Every experience is meant to free us from the entrapment of false attachments and outside conditions as the source for our safety and wellbeing. Through each stage and phase, there will be a gentle nudging to let go and remember that the source of everything is and always will be from within, and the source is and always will be God's unconditional love, both given and received.

Every day, therefore, is an opportunity to allow safety and love to flow through us and then to witness the abundant blessings that can manifest. Every day is truly an invitation from God with a gentle whisper heard from our prayerful heart: "Take nothing for the journey; instead, let me carry you."

This is the endless desire of God every day. The Holy One seeks to share His unfathomable love and power with us, unconditionally, day by day. Every circumstance is meant to release us from the death grip of fear, if we would only remember to choose His light and partnership daily. If we would allow this divine partnership, we would truly and deeply never feel alone or abandoned. We would remember we are always in Him, with Him, and through Him. We would feel safe and loved in all situations. We would enjoy ourselves, others, and the journey so much more. Even through all adversities, we would remember that in Him, with Him, and through Him, we are once again simply learning to let go of where we have been to embrace where we are going within His kingdom without end, on earth and in heaven. Amen, amen, and Amen!

Remedy for learning and letting go:

* Sit quietly with your eyes closed.
* Create an easy rhythm for your breathing and allow all of your attention to be focused on the center of your chest, where you know your heart and soul to be.
* Sense a beautiful, gentle, golden light in the center of your chest that seems to radiate and increase with every inhalation and exhalation.
* Focus upon the pulsating golden light as you allow yourself to imagine a beautiful place where you feel totally free, calm, and safe. This place may be real or imaginary. This place is your safe haven.
* Remain in your safe haven and create as much detail as desired. Feel as if you are really there.
* Remember, every time you are in your safe haven, the holy presence is always there waiting to guide, assist, and comfort you.
* Examine the following concerns and issues and pause to reflect upon any insights or awareness.
* As you are relaxing in your safe haven with the holy presence, allow yourself to focus as completely as possible upon the holy presence.
* Ask, whenever you are comfortable to do so, "Show me Your truth, light, and love."
* Just continue to breathe comfortably and relax, and then, whenever you are ready, ask the following questions:
  - What past or present conditions are I still letting control me?
  - Why am I still stuck in these false sense of security issues or experiences?

- Why do I give over my inner power that You gave to this particular person, place, or thing?
- How can I learn to remember You are the only source, my only source?
- How can I learn to let go, in order to truly be in the wonderful divine partnership with You as You intended?
- Where am I still unwilling to forgive and forget?
- Will you forgive me?

* Help me to feel about myself the way You always unconditionally love me.

* Please help me to remember every day that I am always safe and loved in You, through You, and with You. Thank You!

* Take your time reflecting upon these insights. It is suggested that this process be repeated as often as you feel necessary. It is suggested that you record these reflections in your journal for further review.

For this perishable nature must put on the imperishable, and this mortal nature must put on immortality. When the perishable puts on the imperishable, and the mortal puts on immortality, then shall come to pass the saying that is written:

"Death is swallowed up in victory. O, death, where is thy victory? O, death, where is the sting?"

The sting of death is sin and the power is the law. But thanks be to God, who gives us the victory through our Lord Jesus Christ. Therefore, my beloved brethren, be steadfast, immovable, always

abounding in the work of the Lord, knowing that
in the Lord, your labor is not in vain.

—Corinthians 15:54–58

And so, we remember:

For everything there is a season, and a time
for every matter under heaven:

a time to be born, and a time to die;
a time to plant, and a time to pluck up what
is planted;
a time to kill, and a time to heal;
a time to break down, and a time to build up;
a time to weep, and a time to laugh;
a time to mourn, and a time to dance;
a time to cast away stones, and a time to gather
stones together;
a time to embrace, and a time to refrain from
embracing;
a time to seek, and a time to lose;
a time to keep, and a time to cast away;
a time to reap, and a time to sow;
a time to keep silent, and a time to speak;
a time to love, and a time to hate;
a time for war, and a time for peace.

What gain has the worker from his toil?
I have seen the business that God has given
us to be busy with.
He has made everything beautiful in its time;

Also he has put eternity into man's mind, yet so that he cannot find out what God has done from the beginning to the end.

I know that there is nothing better for them than to be happy and enjoy themselves, as long as they live;

Also that it is God's gift to us that everyone should eat and drink and take pleasure in all his efforts.

—Ecclesiastes 3:1–13